£2.50

Gift Aid Non fiction
£

0 031140 072084

To My Daughters

Alison & Heather

And to all those who love.

Alphabet

by Carol Nowak

C S Nowak

Linocut is a printmaking technique, a variant of a woodcut. A design is cut into a linoleum surface with a sharp knife to create a raised image. The linoleum is inked with a roller and then printed by hand onto paper.